Title Page

The Insider's Guide to Selling Your Yacht: 12 Mistakes to Avoid
A Guide to a Successful Yacht Sale

By Dan Ribeiro, CPYB
Certified Professional Yacht Broker

Copyright Page

© 2024 Dan Ribeiro. All rights reserved.

No part of this publication may be reproduced, distributed, or transmitted in any form or by any means, including photocopying, recording, or other electronic or mechanical methods, without the prior written permission of the author, except in the case of brief quotations embodied in critical reviews and specific other noncommercial uses permitted by copyright law.

For permission requests, write to the author at the address below:

Dan Ribeiro, CPYB

Email: ribeiro.dan@gmail.com

Dedication

To all those who dream of the open sea and the adventure it promises.

And to my family and friends, whose unwavering support has made this journey possible.

Accomplishments

Over the years, I've had the privilege of helping clients buy and sell more than 100 Yachts and participating in four times that number of surveys and trial runs, ranging in size from 36 feet to 50 meters. My journey in the Yachting world began humbly as a Valet at Hyannis Marina in Cape Cod, MA, and through hard work and dedication, I've built a career that allows me to connect people with their dream vessels.

As a Certified Professional Yacht Broker (CPYB) and an active member of the International Yacht Brokers Association (IYBA) and the SuperYacht Society, I've committed myself to upholding the highest standards in the industry. These affiliations have enabled me to stay connected with the latest trends and best practices, ensuring my clients receive the best possible guidance.

I've focused on providing a personalized, client-centered approach throughout my career. My goal has always been to make the buying and selling process as smooth and rewarding as possible, and I'm grateful for the trust my clients have placed in me.

Foreword

Selling a Yacht is often more than just a business transaction; it's a deeply personal experience. Yachts are symbols of freedom, adventure, and luxury—assets that many people hold close to their hearts. As a Certified Professional Yacht Broker with years of experience in the industry, I've seen firsthand how the process of selling a Yacht can be fraught with emotional and financial challenges.

This book is the culmination of everything I've learned throughout my career. It's a practical guide designed to help you confidently navigate the complexities of selling your Yacht. From setting the right price to finding the perfect buyer, I've outlined the 12 most common mistakes that can derail your sale and provided actionable tips to avoid them.

Whether you're selling your first or tenth Yacht, this book's insights will equip you with the knowledge you need to achieve a successful sale. My goal is to help you maximize the value of your Yacht while minimizing the stress and uncertainty that often accompany the selling process.

Thank you for trusting me as your guide on this journey. I'm confident that with the right approach, you'll find that selling your Yacht can be a rewarding experience that sets the stage for your next great adventure.

Dan Ribeiro, CPYB
Certified Professional Yacht Broker
Miami Beach, Florida
August 2024

Introduction

Selling a Yacht is not just a transaction; it's a complex journey that can determine your financial future. Even for experienced Yacht owners, the process can be challenging and complex, involving many factors such as setting the right price, preparing the Yacht for sale, marketing it effectively, and negotiating with potential buyers. Unfortunately, even a single mistake in these areas can significantly impact your chances of achieving a successful sale or cost you hundreds of thousands of dollars.

I created this guide to help you avoid the 12 most common mistakes Yacht owners make when selling their vessels. By understanding these pitfalls and how to prevent them, you can increase your chances of selling your Yacht quickly and at a fair price.

Each chapter of this book will focus on a specific mistake and provide tips and advice on avoiding it. We'll cover everything from setting a realistic price and preparing your Yacht for showings to negotiating with potential buyers and working with a professional Yacht broker.

Whether you're a first-time Yacht seller or a seasoned veteran, this guide will provide the tools and knowledge you need to navigate the often-complicated world of Yacht sales. So, let's get started and help you achieve a successful Yacht sale!

Mistake #1: Overpricing

One of the most common mistakes of yacht owners when selling their vessels is overpricing. While setting a high price to maximize your profits may be tempting, an unrealistic price can deter potential buyers and prolong the selling process.

Why Overpricing is a Mistake:
- **Reduced Interest:** When you overprice your Yacht, it may attract less interest from potential buyers than if you priced it competitively. Buyers are often wary of overpriced vessels and may look for more reasonably priced Yachts.
- **Longer Time on the Market:** The longer your Yacht sits on the market, the less attractive it becomes to potential buyers. Overpricing can lead to a longer time on the market, as buyers may be waiting for the price to drop or looking for alternatives.
- **Lower Final Selling Price:** Overpricing your Yacht can result in a lower final price. The longer your Yacht sits on the market, the more likely you will receive lowball offers from buyers who assume you are eager to sell.

Tips for Pricing Your Yacht Competitively:
- **Research Similar Yachts:** Look at other Yachts like yours and see what they sold for. Pricing your Yacht in line with others in the market will help ensure it moves quickly. The correct price will make the boat move; the wrong price won't.
- **Consider the Condition:** When pricing your Yacht, consider its condition. You may need to lower the price accordingly if it needs repairs or upgrades. Today's buyer is savvy, and 99% of items will be found during the survey
- **Use a Professional Appraiser:** Consider hiring a professional appraiser to determine your Yacht's market value. This can help ensure that you set a fair and accurate price.

Avoiding overpricing your Yacht can increase your chances of attracting potential buyers and achieving a successful sale.

Mistake #2: Poor Cosmetic Condition

Another familiar mistake Yacht owners make when selling their vessels is not ensuring their Yacht is in excellent condition. A poorly maintained Yacht can be a turn-off for potential buyers and may result in a lower selling price.

Example:
Suppose you're selling a 40-foot sailing Yacht that has been in your family for years. The Yacht has not been used often recently, and you have yet to keep up with regular maintenance. As a result, the Yacht has some cosmetic issues, including peeling paint, stained upholstery, and outdated electronics.

If you put this Yacht on the market without any repairs or upgrades, potential buyers will likely be deterred by its poor condition. They may assume that the Yacht needs to be better cared for and may worry about the cost and effort required to bring it up to their standards. As a result, you may receive lower offers than if the Yacht had been in better condition.

Tips for Ensuring Your Yacht is in Excellent Condition:
- **Conduct a Thorough Inspection:** Before listing your Yacht for sale, have it inspected by a professional surveyor. This can help you identify any issues that need to be addressed before putting it on the market.
- **Make Necessary Repairs:** Address any issues identified during the inspection, such as engine problems, leaks, or structural damage. Also, consider cosmetic repairs, such as repainting or replacing worn-out upholstery.
- **Upgrade Outdated Features:** If your Yacht has outdated electronics or other features that may be a turn-off for potential buyers, consider upgrading them. For example, installing a new navigation system or updating the entertainment system can make your Yacht more attractive to buyers.

Ensuring that your Yacht is in excellent condition can increase its appeal to potential buyers and achieve a higher selling price.

Mistake #3: Inadequate Marketing

In today's digital age, over 80% of Yacht buyers use the internet to research and find their next Yacht. However, many Yacht owners need to invest more time and effort into marketing their vessels online. This can lead to a lack of interest from potential buyers and a prolonged selling process.

Example:
Did you know that Yachts with high-quality photos and videos receive up to 3 times more views than those with poor-quality visuals? Additionally, Yachts on multiple websites receive up to 20% more inquiries than those on just one website.

Tips for Effective Marketing:
- **Use High-Quality Photos and Videos:** Ensure your Yacht is showcased with well-lit, high-resolution images and videos highlighting its best features. According to research, listings with high-quality photos receive four times more inquiries than those with low-quality photos.
- **Create a Compelling Listing:** Your listing should be descriptive and compelling, highlighting the Yacht's best features, amenities, and condition. More detailed listings receive up to 50% more inquiries than those that need more detail.
- **Use Multiple Listing Sites:** Don't limit your listing to just one website. Instead, list your Yacht on multiple websites to reach a wider audience. Yachts listed on three or more websites receive up to 60% more inquiries than those listed on only one.
Attend Yacht Shows: According to the National Marine Manufacturers Association, Yacht shows are the most popular venue for Yacht buyers to research and purchase their next Yacht. Consider attending a Yacht show in your area to showcase your Yacht to potential buyers in person.

Investing in effective marketing efforts can significantly increase your Yacht's exposure to potential buyers and achieve a quicker sale at a higher price.

Mistake #4: Misrepresenting the Yacht

Misrepresenting your Yacht can have serious consequences, including legal issues, a damaged reputation, and a prolonged selling process. According to a survey by BoatUS, misrepresenting a Yacht was one of the most common reasons for legal disputes between buyers and sellers.

Example:
Misrepresenting your Yacht's condition can lower its selling price. According to a Yacht Brokers Association of America survey misrepresented Yachts can sell for up to 10% less than their actual value.

Tips for Accurate Representation:
- **Be Honest About the Yacht's Condition:** Be upfront about any issues or necessary repairs your Yacht needs. Consider conducting a professional survey to identify any potential problems.
- **Disclose Any Accidents or Incidents:** If your Yacht has been involved in any accidents or incidents, it's essential to disclose this information to potential buyers to avoid legal issues down the line.
- **Don't Misrepresent Features or Equipment:** Be honest about your Yacht's features and equipment. Misrepresenting these can lead to distrust and potential legal issues.
- **Use Accurate Photos and Videos:** Use photos and videos that accurately represent your Yacht's condition and features. Avoid using old or misleading visuals that could lead to misrepresentation.

By accurately representing your Yacht, you can build trust with potential buyers and achieve a higher selling price.

Mistake #5: Failing to Address Legal Issues

Selling a Yacht involves several legal considerations that can be complex and time-consuming. Failing to address these issues can result in legal disputes, delays in the selling process, and potentially lower selling prices.

Example:
Not properly transferring the title of your Yacht can lead to legal issues down the line. According to a survey by the Boat Owners Association of The United States, title issues were the second most common reason for legal disputes between buyers and sellers.

Tips for Addressing Legal Issues:
- **Verify Your Yacht's Title:** Ensure you have a clear title for your Yacht and that it is properly registered with the appropriate agencies. You can work with a maritime attorney to ensure your Yacht's title is in order.
- **Disclose Any Liens or Encumbrances:** If your Yacht has any liens or encumbrances, it's essential to disclose this information to potential buyers to avoid legal issues down the line.
- **Ensure Compliance with Regulations:** Your Yacht must comply with all relevant regulations and laws, such as Coast Guard requirements, environmental regulations, and tax laws. Failure to comply can result in legal issues and potential fines.
- **Use a Professional Yacht Broker:** Consider working with a professional Yacht broker with experience handling legal issues related to Yacht sales. They can help ensure all legal requirements are met and assist with paperwork and documentation.

Addressing legal issues upfront can help you avoid potential legal disputes and ensure a smoother, more successful Yacht sale.

Mistake #6: Not Preparing for Showings

One of the most common mistakes Yacht owners make when selling their vessels is not preparing the Yacht for showings. A poorly presented Yacht can be a turn-off for potential buyers and may result in a lower selling price.

Example:
Imagine that you are selling a 60-foot Motor Yacht. You invite potential buyers to come on board for a showing, but the Yacht is not clean, organized, or staged adequately for the occasion. The mess may put off the potential buyers, who may need help visualizing themselves owning and enjoying the Yacht.

Tips for Preparing Your Yacht for showings:
- **Clean the Yacht:** Before any showings, ensure the Yacht is clean and clutter-free. This includes cleaning the interior and exterior, removing personal items, and decluttering the Yacht.
- **Stage the Yacht:** Consider staging it to make it more attractive to potential buyers. This may include setting the table for a meal or arranging the deck chairs to showcase the Yacht's outdoor living space.
- **Address Any Minor Repairs:** Address any minor repairs or cosmetic issues before showings. This may include fixing leaky faucets, replacing burned-out light bulbs, or repainting areas that show wear and tear.
- **Create a Positive Environment:** Create a welcoming and positive environment for potential buyers. This may include offering refreshments, playing music, and engaging in friendly conversation.

Properly preparing your Yacht for showings can create a positive first impression and result in a quicker sale at a higher price.

Mistake #7: Lack of Transparency

When selling a Yacht, it is crucial to be transparent with potential buyers about its condition, history, and any relevant information. Failing to provide this information upfront can lead to distrust, legal issues, and a prolonged selling process.

Example:
Imagine you're selling a Yacht involved in a minor collision a few years ago. If you fail to disclose this information to potential buyers and they discover it later, they may feel that you were dishonest and may be less likely to purchase the Yacht.

Tips for Ensuring Transparency:
- **Disclose Any Accidents or Incidents:** Be upfront about any accidents or incidents that your Yacht has been involved in. This includes collisions, groundings, and any other incidents that could impact the Yacht's condition or value.
- **Provide a Detailed History:** Provide potential buyers with a detailed history of your Yacht, including any significant repairs or upgrades and regular maintenance.
- **Answer Questions Honestly:** When potential buyers ask questions about your Yacht, answer them honestly and provide as much information as possible. This can help build trust and ensure a smoother selling process.
- **Use Professional Inspections:** Consider having a professional inspect your Yacht before putting it on the market. This can help identify any potential issues you may need to disclose to potential buyers.

By being transparent with potential buyers, you can avoid legal issues, build trust, and achieve a quicker sale at a higher price.

Mistake #8: Being Too Pushy

When selling a Yacht, it's important to allow potential buyers to make their own decisions without being too pushy or aggressive. Being too pushy can result in a breakdown of trust and a lost sale.

Tips to Avoid Being Too Pushy:
- **Provide Space and Time:** Give potential buyers space and time to explore and consider the Yacht independently. Avoid hovering or pressuring them to make a decision.
- **Be Available for Questions:** Make yourself available to answer any questions potential buyers may have, but avoid pressing them to make a decision.
- **Follow Up Professionally:** Follow up with potential buyers professionally, but avoid being pushy or aggressive. Respect their decision-making process and allow them to reach their own conclusions.

Example:
Imagine you're selling a 60-foot sailing Yacht in the Caribbean. During a showing, a potential buyer seems interested but hesitant to make an offer. Instead of pressuring them to decide, you provide additional information and resources to help them make an informed decision. This patience and professionalism result in a successful sale.

You can build trust with potential buyers and achieve a successful sale by being patient and not being too pushy.

Mistake #9: Not Considering All Offers

When selling a Yacht, it's essential to consider all offers, even if they aren't ideal. Rejecting offers out of hand can result in a longer time on the market and potentially lower selling prices.

Tips for Considering All Offers:
- **Know Your Bottom Line:** Before entering negotiations, know your bottom line—the lowest price you will accept for your Yacht. This will help you stay firm in negotiations and be open to considering other offers.
- **Negotiate Professionally:** Negotiate with potential buyers professionally, even if their offer is lower than your ideal price. Consider offering incentives to sweeten the deal, such as including accessories or electronics with the Yacht.
- **Consider Timing and Market Conditions:** When considering offers, take into account the current market conditions and timing. A lower offer might be more advantageous in a buyer's market or during off-peak seasons.

Example:
Imagine you're selling a Yacht and receive an offer below your asking price. Instead of rejecting it outright, you negotiate professionally and find common ground. This approach leads to a successful sale at a price that meets your expectations.

Mistake #10: Ignoring Feedback

Feedback from potential buyers and brokers can be invaluable in improving your Yacht's marketing and sales strategy. Ignoring feedback can result in a lack of interest from potential buyers and a longer time on the market.

Tips for Using Feedback to Improve Your Sales Strategy:
- **Listen to Feedback:** Take the time to listen to feedback from potential buyers and brokers. Consider their comments and suggestions, even if they differ from what you want.
- **Use Feedback to Improve Marketing Materials:** Use feedback to improve your Yacht's marketing materials, such as photos, videos, and descriptions. Consider what aspects potential buyers found appealing or unappealing and adjust accordingly.
- **Adjust Pricing and Negotiation Strategy:** Use feedback to adjust your Yacht's pricing and negotiation strategy. Consider what potential buyers are focusing on and adjust your bottom line and negotiation tactics accordingly.

Example:
Imagine you're selling a 50-foot power Yacht in California. After multiple showings, several potential buyers have commented on the need for more detail in your marketing materials. In response, you hire a professional photographer and videographer to create high-quality visuals of the Yacht. The improved marketing materials lead to increased interest from potential buyers and a successful sale.

Using feedback to improve your Yacht's sales strategy can increase potential buyers' interest and achieve a successful sale.

Mistake #11: Not Hiring a Professional Broker

Hiring a professional broker can significantly benefit the Yacht-selling process. An experienced broker can provide expertise, industry connections, and guidance throughout selling.

Tips for Finding and Choosing the Right Broker:
- **Research and Interview Multiple Brokers:** Research and interview multiple brokers to find the right fit for your needs. Consider factors such as experience, reputation, and industry connections.
- **Look for a Broker with Specialization:** Look for a broker who sells Yachts like yours. They will better understand the market and potential buyers.
- **Consider Commission Structure:** When choosing a Yacht broker, it's essential to consider their commission structure. A reputable and experienced broker typically charges a standard commission rate of around 10%, which is split between the broker representing the buyer and the broker representing the seller. Avoid brokers who offer lower commission rates, as this can hinder co-brokerage opportunities and limit your Yacht's exposure to potential buyers.

Example:
Imagine a Yacht owner in Miami who hired a captain who was also a broker to sell their Yacht. However, the captain was often out at sea, leaving potential buyers to call multiple times without receiving a response. One possible buyer called the following Yacht listing and purchased a different boat instead.

This example highlights the importance of hiring a reputable, experienced broker who can effectively communicate with potential buyers and provide the necessary attention and expertise to market the Yacht and achieve a successful sale.

Mistake #12: Rushing the Sale

Rushing the sale process can result in a lack of interest from potential buyers and a lower selling price. Taking the necessary time to prepare the Yacht and find the right buyer can result in a more successful sale.

Tips for Avoiding Rushing the Sale:
- **Take the Time to Prepare the Yacht:** Take the time to prepare the Yacht for sale, including repairs, maintenance, and cleaning. A well-prepared Yacht can attract more potential buyers and result in a higher selling price.
- **Be Patient:** Take the time to find the right buyer. Rushing the sale can result in lower prices or legal disputes later.
- **Allow Time for Negotiations:** Allow time for negotiations with potential buyers. Rushing negotiations can result in a breakdown of trust and potentially lost sales.

Example:
Imagine you're selling a 65-foot sailing Yacht in Cape Cod. Instead of rushing through the sale process, you take the time to prepare the Yacht for sale, including performing necessary repairs and having it professionally cleaned. You also allow time for negotiations with potential buyers and ultimately find the right buyer, resulting in a successful sale.

Taking the necessary time to prepare the Yacht and find the right buyer can make the sale more successful.

Conclusion

Selling a Yacht is different from selling any ordinary item. It is a complex process that requires specialized knowledge, experience, and skills to navigate successfully. A Yacht is a high-value asset, and the selling process involves various legal, financial, and technical aspects that can be daunting and time-consuming for an individual without the necessary expertise.

Hiring a professional Yacht broker can significantly simplify the selling process and increase your chances of achieving a successful sale. Yacht brokers are experts in the Yacht market and possess a wealth of knowledge and experience in Yacht sales. They have access to extensive market data, enabling them to determine the optimal pricing for your Yacht, considering its features, condition, and current market trends.

Moreover, Yacht brokers have established networks of industry connections, including other brokers, buyers, and Yacht manufacturers, which they can leverage to market your Yacht to a broader audience. They also have the resources to create effective marketing materials, such as high-quality photos and videos, and promote your Yacht through various channels, including print and digital media, boat shows, and industry events.

Perhaps most importantly, a Yacht broker is an experienced negotiator who can help you get the best possible deal for your Yacht. They can handle all aspects of the negotiation process, including counteroffers contingencies.

, and legal documents, ensuring your interests are protected throughout the sale.

Attempting to sell a Yacht on your own or hiring an unprofessional broker can result in costly mistakes, legal disputes, a lower selling price, and a longer time on the market. Therefore, choosing a reputable and experienced Yacht broker who can guide you through the entire selling process and help you achieve a fair and successful sale is crucial.

In conclusion, selling a Yacht is a complex and challenging process that requires specialized knowledge, expertise, and skills. Hiring a professional Yacht broker can significantly simplify the process and increase your chances of a successful sale. With their industry connections, market knowledge, marketing skills, and negotiation expertise, a reputable Yacht broker can help you navigate the complexities of the selling process and achieve a fair and successful sale.

Acknowledgments

I want to extend my heartfelt thanks to @theyachtmentor,fellow brokers, Yacht owners, and industry professionals who have been instrumental in shaping my career and helping me write this book. Your insights, knowledge, and generosity have been invaluable, and I am grateful for all you have taught me.

To my fellow brokers, thank you for being my colleagues, competitors, and friends. Your professionalism, dedication, and passion for Yachts have inspired me to become a better broker and person.

To all the Yacht owners who have entrusted me with selling their vessels, thank you for your trust, confidence, and support. It has been a privilege to work with you and help you achieve your Yachting dreams.

To all the industry professionals who have shared their expertise and knowledge with me, thank you for your generosity and support. Your insights and advice have been invaluable, and I am grateful for all you have taught me.

Finally, I would like to thank my family and friends for their love, encouragement, and support throughout the writing of this book. Your belief in me has driven my success, and I am grateful for all you do.

Thank you all for being a part of my journey. This book is dedicated to you, and I deeply appreciate and appreciate your support.

Sources

- National Marine Manufacturers Association (2019). "Yacht Market Data: What You Need to Know." Accessed on March 8, 2023.
https://www.nmma.org/sites/default/files/2019-06/Yacht%20Market%20Data%20-%20What%20You%20Need%20to%20Know.pdf
- Forbes (2018). "The Art of Selling a Yacht: Tips from Industry Experts." Accessed on March 8, 2023.
https://www.forbes.com/sites/marjoriecohen/2018/05/03/the-art-of-selling-a-Yacht-tips-from-industry-experts/?sh=607186f75617
- YachtWorld (2022). "10 Mistakes to Avoid When Selling Your Boat." Accessed on March 8, 2023.
https://www.Yachtworld.com/blog/10-mistakes-to-avoid-when-selling-your-boat/
- Boat International (2022). "How to Sell a Yacht: Tips for a Successful Sale." Accessed on March 8, 2023.
https://www.boatinternational.com/Yacht-market-intelligence/brokerage-advice/how-to-sell-a-Yacht--41408

Made in the USA
Middletown, DE
10 September 2024